The Dangers of Chloroform and the Safety and Efficiency of Ether As an Agent in Securing the Avoidance of Pain in Surgical Operations, with a Description of an Ether Inhaler

John Morgan

THE

DANGERS OF CHLOROFORM

AND THE

SAFETY AND EFFICIENCY

OF

ETHER,

AS AN AGENT IN

SECURING THE AVOIDANCE OF PAIN

IN

SURGICAL OPERATIONS.

By J. MORGAN, M.D., F.R.C.S.,
Professor of Surgical and Descriptive Anatomy, Royal College of Surgeons, Ireland; Surgeon to Mercer's Hospital, Dublin, etc.

WITH

A DESCRIPTION OF AN ETHER INHALER,

AND THE MODE OF ADMINISTRATION.

LONDON:
BAILLIÈRE, TINDALL, AND COX,
20 KING WILLIAM STREET, STRAND.

MDCCCLXXII.

LONDON:
PRINTED BY BAILLIERE, TINDALL AND COX,
KING WILLIAM STREET.

PREFACE.

In drawing attention to the subject of the Dangers of the Use of Chloroform, when compared with the Advantages and Safety of the Use of Ether, in producing insensibility to pain, I am influenced by having practically observed the difficulties, and witnessed the anxieties inseparable from its use, which oppress the Surgeon when undertaking an operation.

In addition, on impartially and calmly reviewing the subject, and analysing the experience of years, I find that Ether has infinitely superior claims as to *Safety* and Efficiency.

Great Britain and America have each produced their national anæsthetics, Chloroform being the child of the former, and Ether of the latter. We find that Chloroform, which since 1848 has been largely used in this country, is still looked on with a certain amount of suspicion and distrust by the majority of practitioners; and that the most scrupulous directions and abundant warnings are given by writers, to prevent any accidental complication which might increase an already fully recognised danger.

Ether, on the other hand, which has stood the test since 1846, has been the American favourite, and so far from any timidity or hesitation accompanying its use, such is the confidence reposed in it, that it is stated by the very most recent authority on Surgical Practice (*a*), that "a patient cannot be too rapidly etherized, and there is no danger, as in the case of Chloroform, from the vapour being too concentrated."

Yet, notwithstanding the extra care engendered by timidity on the one hand, and the boldness engendered by confidence on the other, the result of statistical information is remarkable, and is well calculated to call into question the tendency to conservatism which we incline to, professionally, as well as nationally, in so persisting in the use of Chloroform, notwithstanding its obvious danger.

It is a startling fact to find that by the latest statistics of both Great Britain and America,—taking only the deaths directly accredited to the use of anæsthetics—it is proved that

Chloroform is eight times more dangerous than Ether, and is the most dangerous of all the anæsthetics in use (*b*).

Such being the ascertained ratio from published

(*a*) Asshurst, November, 1871.

(*b*) One death a week, is said to be the average in this country.

accidents, let any Surgeon ask himself how many escapes he has witnessed,—how often he has seen stimulants and the means of resuscitation applied even to the extreme measures of the use of galvanism and of restoring suspended animation,—how often he has seen operations completed without the full influence of Chloroform,—how often his attention has been diverted from the immediate concern of his operation to the condition of the patient, due to the influence of Chloroform,—and how often he feared to administer it at all; he will no doubt subscribe to the verdict of the London Chloroform Committee, that an "agent is desired which is not so dangerous in its operation as Chloroform."

As Ether represents such an agent, more so than any as yet discovered, I am desirous of drawing attention to its advantages and superiority; and when I find that but 1 death in 23,204 Ether inhalations can be ascertained as at all attributable to its use, I believe that a ratio representing merely an infinitesimal risk, has been thus attained; and that by using Ether as a pain-destroyer, instead of the patient entering upon an operation with the sword of Damocles suspended over him, as with Chloroform; he will sink more calmly, and infinitely more safely, into insensibility, relying with confidence on the mystic power of the Anæsthetic, the skill of the Surgeon, and the goodness of his Maker, in obtaining relief from his sufferings.

I have arranged an Anæsthetic Inhaler, which

I find most convenient, safe, and effectual; it is so constructed that by means of a mouth-piece with a flexible tube, operations about the face can be performed with ease, while the lulling influence of the Etherization is perfectly secured, and the abundant and rapid evaporation of the ethereal vapour is attained and directly applied

23 St. Stephen's Green, North,
Dublin.

"Deaths from Chloroform are now so frequent (it has been said one in a week), and we are told that many deaths from this cause are never reported at all, that the time is not far distant when the public safety will demand some inquiry into the use of this deadly agent, more comprehensive than anything hitherto done in that way" (a).

(a) Mr. Greene, in *British Medical Journal.*

THE

DANGERS OF CHLOROFORM.

THE SAFETY OF ETHER AS A PAIN-DESTROYER.

SINCE the all-important era of the introduction of anæsthetics into surgical practice, and the invaluable boon of the avoidance of pain, whether in small or large operations; claims have at times been set forth in favour of various means of attaining this desirable end—chloroform, ether, a mixture of both, nitrous oxide gas, &c., have had their advocates; and the great object of producing a temporary state of insensibility has been achieved by any one of these agents. Chloroform, undoubtedly, in these countries, has as yet carried the palm, and has had the most ample use. No one who has either witnessed or experienced its value in the extinction of pain, can possibly doubt its efficacy, or can question the honours and laudations which have been bestowed upon the late Sir J. Simpson as the introducer of this agent into practice; but in order to attain the state of "suspended sensation," even in small operations, and, in addition, to retain this condition for a length of time, as is necessary in some of the larger and more tedious proceedings of surgery; the gauntlet of certain dangers, unfortunately, has to be run, which every practical surgeon will candidly admit, cause him much anxiety, and, I think I may add, in many instances impress him with responsibility, far *more* than the operation in which he is about to engage.

The very appointment of special and skilled "chloroformists" to large institutions, and the anxiety felt that a medical examination should be carefully made as to the condition of the heart and other organs of a patient about being operated on, lest any accident from chloroform should arise; proves the "*arrière pensée*" which admittedly exists in the minds of surgeons as to its *dangers.* How few would undertake the performance of even a simple operation, which involved the use of chloroform, without guarding against its risks, or without having by him the recognised means of restoring animation, and being prepared to apply them according to the emergency of the case, from the use of stimulants even to the last and critical resource of keeping up artificial respiration, as in ordinary instances of suffocation. Indeed, it must be admitted that in proceeding to operate, the surgeon should be accompanied not only by his assistants, but by a chloroformist, and the latter again should be furnished with the necessary means of combatting, not the results of the operation, but of the agent he is intrusted to administer, necessitating as it does an admission of responsibility, and of an inseparable amount of hazard, as proved by the arrangement of stimulants —ammonia, the galvanic battery, &c., so as to be at hand when required.

The *danger* of chloroform is an admitted one by the Profession, and is anxiously questioned by the Public. The chapters devoted to its consideration, and to the discussion of the use of "Anæsthesia in Surgery," by writers prove that, while chloroform stands as yet foremost in use in these countries, it has its inseparable difficulties, its dangers, and its anxieties.

The column "Death by Chloroform" is not unfilled, and the reports of coroners' inquests, where death has been attributed to such cause, do not fail to produce so painful an impression of distrust on the public mind that a patient who has undergone its influence, will at times recall his sensations in Endymion's words.

> "Long in misery
> I wasted, ere in one extremest fit
> I plunged for life or death."

When to the *deaths* by chloroform, we add those not unfrequent chloroform accidents, where artificial respiration alone restored the patient, where life was hovering on extinction, and where the faintest attempt at respiration was so anxiously watched for, and heard with such intense relief (though such cases do not come under immediate publicity), it must indeed be admitted they would tend very much to intensify the distrust which is more or less acknowledged, and is the real impediment of this "pain destroyer," when we are about, by its means, to use the words of a modern surgical writer (*a*), reducing the patient to a condition in "which, to the uninitiated, he appears in *articulo mortis*," and in "which very little more would place the circumstances in a most critical relation."

So important had the question of *death by chloroform* finally become, even in 1864, that a Committee was appointed by the Royal Medical and Chirurgical Society of London to inquire into the uses, and the Physiological, Therapeutical, and Toxical effects of Chloroform.

(*a*) Miller's "Surgery," p. 58[illegible].

This Committee, composed of most eminent and pains-taking observers, while investigating the subject of Chloroform, indirectly considered the use of Ether, which had been the first anæsthetic largely employed, and which is still employed in its birthplace, America, more largely, and far more successfully, than Chloroform.

The accompanying tabular comparison gives a summary of the general conclusions arrived at by this Chloroform Committee, with regard to the comparative *dangers* of Chloroform and Ether on the two chief functions of life—the circulation and respiration.

It is interesting, as showing the more *immediate* interference of Chloroform with them, and how easily, under any accident, a fatal issue might arise. We find as follows:—

EFFECT OF ETHER INHALATION.	EFFECT OF CHLOROFORM INHALATION.
The Heart.	*The Heart*
The muscular movement is but little influenced. The first or stimulating effect is less sudden, and more sustained. Even after insensibility is procured, its action is more vigorous. Ether may be considered as a stimulant in a certain degree to the heart's action. The mercury of the hæmadynamometer at first is absolutely raised—never falling till the respirations cease.	Is first stimulated, and its contraction force augmented; but, after this, its action is depressed and, although the respirations go on properly, its action, as shown by the mercury of the hæmadynamometer when connected with the circulation of the animal, fails; and the mercury falls.
The Respiration.	*The Respiration.*
With strong inhalation there is a temporary arrest of respiration, but it is less marked than with chloro-	With strong inhalation there is a temporary arrest of respiration dependent on spasm. This arrest, after

form. With small quantities there is no arrest of the breathing, although the number and depth of the respiratory efforts are diminished; after a short time the respirations become slow and full, and next, while their frequency rises, the range of their movements is reduced.

a few seconds, ceases, and inhalation can again take place; with smaller quantities the inspirations become gradually shallower, and for a time retain their natural order, but become less frequent; and after perfect insensibility is produced, the amount of air entering the chest is extremely small.

How it Arrested Life.

The effects produced in a strong quantity, equalled those of chloroform in a small, but with an important contrast, that it exerted but a very slight depressing influence on the heart. Death occurred by the failure of the respiratory movements—the heart's pulsations continuing generally for sometime after the respiration has ceased.

How it Arrested Life.

Strong inhalation caused the pulse and respiration to cease nearly simultaneously. In the majority of cases the pulse stopped before the respiration, and the heart's action could be distinguished for some time after the pulse had ceased.

The conclusion formed by the Committee was, "that it is desirable to obtain an agent which shall produce the required insensibility, and yet is not so dangerous in its operation as Chloroform.

"Ether, to a certain extent, fulfils these conditions: *it is less dangerous than chloroform;* but its odour is disagreeable: it is slow in operation, and it gives rise to greater excitement than chloroform." The Committee, therefore, admit the comparatively *greater danger* of Chloroform, while Ether is objected to, but for the three *inconveniences* mentioned.

The Committee states that "the only apparatus known for Chloroform administration, which fulfils the necessary conditions, is that contrived by Mr. Clover; but at the same time it is open to objections," which can be easily understood, of non-portability, &c. Although the admixture of air is obtained by its means, yet even then the members state that, "with every care, and with the most exact dilution of the chloroform vapour, the state of insensibility may pass *in a few moments into one of imminent death!*"

Dr. Ellis, in his treatise, 1866, since published, throws considerable doubt on the possibility of an even admixture of air and chloroform being attained by any instrument in use at the time of the Report of the Commission.

On examining the Report of the Commission, June, 1864, a table of 123 deaths occurring "during, or immediately after, the administration of chloroform," is recorded—109 deaths being thus given :—

Under 5 years - -	0
From 5 to 15 years -	9
From 15 to 30 „ -	30
From 30 to 45 „ -	32
From 45 to 60 „ -	12
Over 60 years - -	2

72 cases were in males, and 32 in females.

Many other dubious cases, no doubt, might be enrolled in this category; but for obvious reasons, deaths from Chloroform may be, pardonably almost, excused recording.

But when at that date so many were admittedly due to its influence, how many more, it may be fairly asked, have occurred since?

On the other hand, Ether admittedly is comparatively free from this very unpleasant accident. I am assured by Dr. Godon, late Resident Surgeon at Charity and Bellevue

Hospitals, New York, that he has, during the last four years, seen and assisted at thousands of cases of Etherization where, while the most satisfactory results were obtained, not the slightest accident occurred, nor was in any way anticipated. The usual "armamenta" accompanying the chloroformist, of stimulants, galvanic apparatus, &c., being absolutely unheard of.

I have myself frequently *Etherized* and operated on several patients a day with the most satisfactory results, and the most comfortable sense of security, as compared with Chloroform, justifying almost the observation of M. Diday in the recent discussion on another death by Chloroform at the Société de Médecine, Lyons, which puts the matter in so strong a light, that the advantage of Ether as "less dangerous than Chloroform" must command attention.

The *Gazette Médicale de Paris*, July 13, states:—"A case of death from Chloroform has just been reported, which occurred May 27th. Professor Billroth was proceeding to amputate at the hip-joint—the femoral artery had been tied—and he was about to divide the soft parts with the galvano-cautery, when the breathing became stertorous. Tracheotomy was performed, the windpipe opened without delay, and the other means used for reanimation, but all was useless—the patient was dead." Another case of death by Chloroform, during an amputation of the thigh, was given by M. Cabasse to the Société de Médecine at Lyons.

The Society then entered into the discussion of the comparative merits of Ether and Chloroform as anæsthetic agents; when, for the third time, the Society pronounced in favour of *Etherization.*

In Lyons the generality of surgeons employ Ether to the exclusion of Chloroform. Some surgeons there, however, still were in favour of Chloroform. M. Diday proposed the adoption of conclusions by the Society so strong as that "Chloroform is dangerous, and that the surgeons who use it are culpable;" which, in fact, would be a foregone condemnation of any surgeon who used it, should a death occur while under its influence. A Commission of Enquiry was formed by the Medical Society, and a report by M. Valette of the conclusions arrived at was read. Subsequently, the Society hesitated to take upon itself the responsibility of adopting the sweeping proposal of M. Diday, and limited itself to pronouncing *in favour of Etherization*, and admitting that the comparative study of the two anæsthetics was far from being complete.

The Society voted the permanent sitting of the commission on the subject for further investigations.

The report of the London Commission of 1864 states "That the sequence of the phenomena during the experiments on animals is similar to that observed in man, and if the same percentage of the agent be administered, the results produced are nearly uniform." Much valuable information may, therefore, be obtained by comparative testings on animals, they are of so simple and reassuring a nature that a performance of them will go far to show the superiority of Ether as an anæsthetic agent, leaving the triple argument of "disagreable odour," "greater liability to cause excitement," and "its greater tediousness," to be further discussed and observed upon; objections, which seem to me so insignificant, even if we admit them as compared with *danger to life*, that I cannot believe they could for a moment be of weight.

I noted this day four patients I etherized. One, a very strong man, where extraction of a cataract (*a*) was performed. Insensibility was obtained in ten minutes; the pulse remained steady; there was no sickness of stomach; and the operation was most successfully and happily terminated—just as in a similar case which I etherized a few days previously.

Another vigorous patient, of 17, in four and half minutes sank quietly into insensibility with the most perfect result; pulse from 80 to 86; respirations increased six per minute. I occupied about five minutes in operating; and the patient emerged from insensibility equably and gently—there was no excitement or sickness.

Another, of 24, became influenced in ten minutes, with no excitement beyond bursts of laughter; there was no sickness of stomach. I occupied five minutes in operating; the recovery was most equable.

Another, of 30, became influenced in eight minutes, and fully so in ten minutes, with no excitement or approximation to convulsions, and no sickness. I occupied six minutes in operating.

In the last case I had used Chloroform three times previously, and Ether once; and in the second last case I had used Chloroform five times, and Ether once. In both, but in the second last more particularly, the convulsive stage under the use of Chloroform was always very severe and protracted.

Ether produced *incomparably* superior results in every way, accompanied by a sense of much greater security. I particularly noted these instances, as I had observed the previous effects of Chloroform on the patients.

It is but natural that we should examine with attention

(*a*) By Dr. Jacob.

the expressed opinions of surgeons as to an agent which has been most used in America, the country which may be allowed to have been the birthplace of the application of anæsthetics in surgical practice. Since the time when Dr. Morton, so long since as 1846, introduced its use as a "pain-destroyer," Ether has stood the test for the period which has since elapsed, and it is still, in that country, the more universally adopted means of obtaining insensibility.

I find in the last very accurate surgical work which has issued from the press, 1871, the question of Ether *versus* Chloroform is thus reviewed (*a*) :—

"Chloroform is more prompt in its effects; the patient is usually quieter while coming under its influence; it is less apt to cause vomiting; a smaller quantity suffices to produce anæsthesia, and the patient reacts more quickly when the inhalation is stopped. It, however, requires greater care in its administration than Ether, and its use is attended *with much greater risk to life!* This statement gives my own estimate of the relative merits of these agents, and I believe corresponds pretty closely with the opinions usually entertained on the subject. It is right, however, to state that Dr. Lente and Dr. Squibb, of New York, believe that anæsthesia may be induced by means of Ether, as quickly as can safely be done by means of Chloroform, and with a quantity costing less, and weighing very little more than the requisite amount of the latter; and other writers have maintained that vomiting is, at least, as frequently caused by Chloroform as by Ether."

In support of the latter observation, I myself can refer to the cases I have just witnessed, and that in the last

(*a*) "Principles and Practice of Surgery." By J. Ashhurst. P. 75.

thirty patients I etherized within ten days, sickness of stomach occurred but in two, and in these instances, some food had been taken one hour and a half before operation.

"For my own part," says Dr. Asshurst, "I confess *I prefer Ether* in a very large majority of cases; it is certainly, I think, *safer* than Chloroform, and is sufficiently convenient for almost every case that the surgeon is called upon to treat. There is *no danger*, as in the case of Chloroform, of the vapour being too concentrated; indeed, some surgeons, as Dr. Lente, endeavour to prevent even the slightest admixture of air" (*a*).

We have thus reported, by the most recent authority, the value of the arguments for either Chloroform or Ether, "*Safety to life*" and the avoidance of those very unpleasant accidents, "deaths by Chloroform," presenting the strongest claims in favour of Etherisation, and justifying the candid remark of Mr. Erichsen (*b*), of London, when he states,—"The fatal consequences which have attended the employment of Chloroform, have caused American surgeons almost entirely to trust to Ether in preference. Ether is certainly a *safer* agent than Chloroform, but few deaths having resulted from its administration; and the only argument in favour of the use of Chloroform rather than Ether is, that Chloroform is the most *convenient* agent! its effects being produced more quickly, and no disagreeable smell being left, as in the case of Ether." Fortified with such an opinion from so eminent an authority as Mr. Erichsen, M. Diday would be well supported in passing the condemnatory resolution I have already referred to, "that any surgeon using Chloroform instead of Ether as an anæsthetic would be culpable."

(*a*) "Principles and Practice of Surgery." By J. Asshurst, pp. 75-77.
(*b*) "Science and Art of Surgery," p. 17. London, 1869.

Surely, it would be a small solace to a husband for the death of a wife, or to a wife for that of a husband, to be told that Chloroform, which caused the loss of what was held most dear, was used, simply because, while it was far more dangerous, "it was more convenient." Indeed, in a case of death by Chloroform, it appears to me that legal, if not moral culpability might be strenuously urged against the administrator, for using an agent admittedly *more dangerous* than another, simply on the ground as stated, and "the only argument" in its favour, that it was "*more convenient.*" The question is thus becoming daily more serious and debatable.

The late American War furnished enormous opportunities of testing the merits of Ether. In one of the most recent and critical treatises on Military Surgery (*a*), the preference is given to Ether, supported amongst other arguments by the fact that, taking the reports of the General Hospital (Mass.), for ten years, 1850 to 1860, where Ether was exclusively used, "notwithstanding the greater severity of the cases (mostly railroad and street accidents) and the more crowded condition of the hospitals, the average mortality was substantially the same as *before* its introduction. This testimony demonstrates the *superiority of Ether* as compared with Chloroform. "Ether, ought generally to be preferred to Chloroform as being less liable to destroy life immediately."

Few more cogent arguments could be collected than this ten years' epitome of the successful result of Ether, when it is remembered that these cases did not even occur in military practice, where healthy and active soldiers were

(*a*) Dr. Hamilton, Professor of Military Surgery, Bellevue Hospital, New York, p. 621.

the unfortunate sufferers, but in a general hospital, where cases of all varieties, and in diverse circumstances of life, were encountered. It may also be admitted that operations were undertaken with the assistance of Etherization, which, previous to its introduction, would have been unattempted ; yet, while pain was absolved by this "comparatively, though not absolutely, innocuous agent," as styled by Prof. Hamilton, the statistics prove that it in no way contributed to an increased mortality rate.

On inquiring as to the recent practice in the large American institutions, I find in the excellent and compendious Reports of the Boston City Hospital, 1870—including 1,113 operations on in-patients, and 1,062 on out-patients—that amongst all those reported, with such critical procedures as excision of the upper jaw, œsophagotomy, ligature of large arteries, including that of the arteria innominata, excision of the hip-joint, amputations, &c., Ether alone was invariably used, and no ill-consequence or apprehension has been noticed.

In Bellevue Hospital, New York, with something like 1,800 beds, Chloroform has never been used for the last four years, with the many hundreds of operations necessarily constantly performed there. In the Charity Hospital, Blackwell's Island, New York, where Etherization alone is used constantly, not hundreds, but thousands of cases have been submitted to its influence without one *contretemps*. This I have the authority of the Resident Officer for stating, as he himself administered the Ether in a very large number of these patients (*a*) ; while, on the other hand, in the cases in which he saw Chloroform used namely, two cases of hernia, one of hare-lip, and one for

(*a*) Dr. Godon.

repair of a bitten-off nose, there was always much reason for apprehension, and he witnessed the death of one of the patients from the effect of the Chloroform, which was being given where an operation, though painful, but no way involving life (the formation of a nose), was about being performed; it was never commenced, as the patient, a strong healthy looking woman, of 35, died on the operating table, notwithstanding all the means anxiously and actively used for reanimation.

Dr. Mott is said to have preferred Chloroform to Ether (*a*). Evidently, however, Dr. Mott failed to leave the impress of his preference behind him, as in neither of these Institutions—to both of which he was attached—has anything but Ether ever been used since his death. I have obtained the summary of one very remarkable case of a large aneurism of the thoracic aorta, treated by galvano-puncture, at New York Charity Hospital, when Ether was used on several occasions, without any ill consequences, and with a feeling of perfect safety, where Chloroform would have been inadmissible. It is so remarkable that I append it in illustration.

" Bridget Dillon, aged 57, an Irish woman, and comparatively strong; suffering from a large thoracic aneurism; submitted to the attempt of obtaining occlusion by the galvano-puncture; she was Etherized, and came under its influence in about eight minutes; needles were introduced through the chest into the tumour, and connected with a current of seventeen cells. There was no pain or ill consequence whatever. On one occasion the use of the needle was tried *without* Ether; but the pain was excruciating beyond endurance.

(*a*) Hamilton's "Military Surgery," p. 612.

The whole question of the comparative use of the various anæsthetics has been lately very fully reviewed by Dr. W. Coles, who read an elaborate paper replete with overwhelming evidence, at the Medical Society of Virginia, this last session. The arguments in favor of Ether *versus* Chloroform are unanswerable when the great question of *danger to life* is considered. By combining the American statistics, collected by Dr. Andrews, of Chicago, and those of England, by Dr. Richardson, of London, we obtain the following general view of the absolute and relative mortality caused by the several anæsthetic agents in use :—

Agent employed.	Deaths. Inhalations.	Or,
Ether	4 to 92,815	1 to 23,204
Chloroform ...	53 to 152,260	1 to 2,873
Mixture of Chloroform and Ether	2 to 11,176	1 to 5,588
Bichloride Methylene ...	2 to 10,000	1 to 5,000

These figures the author regards as the most valuable and reliable that have ever been published in reference to the *mortality* in anæsthesia. They demonstrate a state of facts so absolutely at variance with the received opinions of five years ago, as *to become perfectly startling.* They indicate that—

Chloroform is eight times more dangerous than Ether;

Twice as dangerous as a mixture of Chloroform and Ether;

And, as far as experience goes, it is

More dangerous than Bichloride of Methylene.

In view of these facts the question arises, Will Chloroform maintain its present popularity as an anæsthetic in surgery? We do not believe it will; unless some method, other than we have at present, is devised to lessen the risk dependent on its use; we cannot but think its popularity must decline. In the face of such figures as adduced, *Chloroform cannot, and ought not to, supersede Ether.* The inconveniences attending the use of Ether are more than compensated for in the risks from Chloroform (*a*).

Nothing can put the question in a plainer light. One death from Ether in 23,204 cases, reduces the risk to a nominal amount.

It is to be recollected that in Etherization there is not the constant and harassing danger ever present; the surgeon is freed from the anxiety that more or less accompanies him into the operating chamber, and his attention can be altogether devoted to the operative procedure in which he is immediately engaged, not, as is too frequently the case, distracted by inquiries as to the condition of the patient, and the influence which the chloroform is exciting. Friends who are intensely interested, are relieved from an additional cause of anxiety which the occasional notice of "Death by Chloroform" may have impressed them with, while equal, if not greater, security of the avoidance of pain is secured, with *Eight times less danger.* Facts such as these cannot fail "to become perfectly startling," and deeply to impress a patient about precipitating himself into the mysterious sleep of insensibility.

With such convincing statistics from the mother country of anæsthetics, where Ether is used, and from Great

(*a*) Hay's *American Journal*, April, 1872, p. 488.

Britain, where Chloroform was introduced and is used,—with the opinion expressed in the latest standard work (*a*) from the former country, of unalterable faith in the use of Ether,—with the opinion, also, of the author of a standard work (*b*) in great Britain, where, though Chloroform is the more largely used, its danger is admitted, and the only argument adduced in its favour is that of convenience; in the face of the discussion at present being agitated on the Continent (*c*), and with the occasional reports which crop up of deaths from Chloroform, the dangers of Chloroform, and the hairbreadth escapes from Chloroform, it is evident that its popularity must wane when calmly contrasted with Ether as an anæsthetic agent.

The surgeon who makes use of Chloroform will employ an agent not only *eight times more dangerous* than Ether, but actually the *most* dangerous of the other agents in use.

Should he not have put these issues before the patient, and should any casualty occur, his responsibility may be indeed seriously brought into question.

(*a*) Asshurst.
(*b*) Erichsen.
(*c*) Société de Médecine.

THE
PULSE WRITING IN ETHERIZATION.

The critical examination into the comparative merits of Ether and Chloroform which I have already referred to, as conducted by the Committee of Investigation appointed by the Royal Medical Chirurgical Society of London, resulted in important observations.

The inquiry was aided by the use of the hemadynamometer in testing the effect of the heart's action and of the influence of these agents upon it. The report states—"The essential difference between the action of Chloroform and of Ether is to be found in the effect produced upon the heart. The first operation of both agents is to stimulate the heart and augment the force of its contractions; but, after this, Chloroform *depresses* the heart's action, whereas Ether appears to exert but little influence upon the muscular movements of that organ." The general accuracy of this remark, though tested by so comparatively coarse an instrument, is borne out by observation of the pulse writing as indicated by the Sphygmograph, an instrument of far greater delicacy which has been since introduced into practice; it affords direct instruction in comparing the influence of Etherization on the pulse, with the healthy condition, by the evidence of the writing.

The accompanying outline of the principle of the Sphygmograph, will serve to explain briefly its mode of action, as writing from the natural soft pulse:—

Fig. 1.

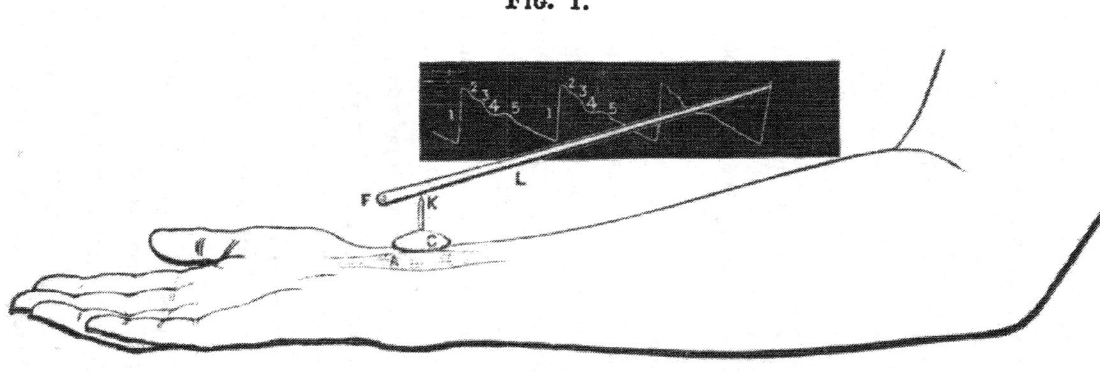

a. The pulse, showing the artery in the act of pulsation.

c. k. The stem, whch communicates its pulsations by being laid on the wrist.

f. l. The index, or pen, which marks the pulsations on a slip of paper, or glass, which receives the writing by being worked along by a rack and spring.

"The writing is that of a natural soft pulse after exercise and residence in the country." (*a*)

(*a*) Dr. Sanderson.

On examining a pulse writing, the component motions may be thus analysed—

Vis a tergo.
1. The First Ascent. Due to the jerk, by the propelling heart.
2. The Indentation. Due to the elastic re-action of the blood-vessel itself.
3. The Elevation. Due to the continued force of the heart's contraction, sending on the blood fluid.

4. The Break. Due to the sudden stopping off, of the heart's action by the valves shutting.
5. The Second Elevation. Due to the action of the blood-vessel itself.

It has already been shown by the Chloroform Committee above quoted, that Ether exercises a stimulating effect on the heart's action, instead of the depressing and sometimes fatal one of Chloroform. It therefore follows that sphygmographic delineations, or pulse writings, should give some aid, as typyfying the immediate effect of Etherization on the heart itself. If the general influence of the "vis a tergo" due to the immediate propulsion of the blood from the heart be understood, in causing the asçent of the pulse writing, with its succeeding fulness or distension, such evidence will be interesting, as showing the condition and vigour of the heart's action during the sleep of Etherization.

In order to simplify the general conclusions as to the value of the indications, I add a bird's-eye view of some of the modifications of pulse writings in various diseased conditions—more particularly with regard to the indications due to the "*vis a tergo*," or immediate influence of the heart.

Typical pulse writings of opposite characters will be instructive. Thus—taking an example of enlargement of the heart (Fig. 2). The high elevation of the pulse writing is remarkable, compared with the undulatory score of typhus fever (Fig. 3), or again with the feeble indications of the flickering heart of a patient worn out by consumption, given during the last hour of life (Fig. 4).

FIG. 2.

Pulse Writing given by an Enlarged Heart.

FIG. 3.

Pulse Writing in Typhus Fever.

FIG. 4.

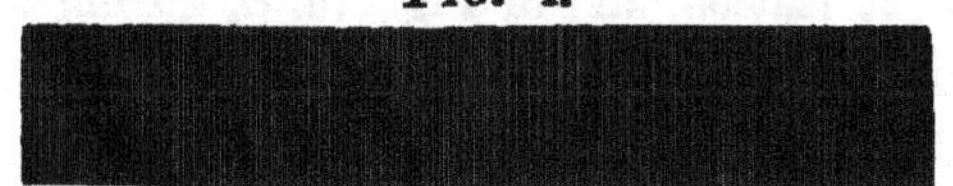

The feeble Pulse Writing of an Expiring Heart.

If these be compared with the copy of a writing given by the "Natural soft pulse after exercise and residence in the country," as shown in Fig. 1, the relative conditions and indications may be estimated.

The following specimens of pulse writing, taken both previous to, and during Etherization, prove that the effect on the heart was that already mentioned by the Chloroform Committee in 1864—

"That Ether was a stimulant to its action."

Fig. 5. represents the pulse of a female patient, aged 25, who had been confined to bed for five months; pulse writing taken before Etherization.

Fig. 6. represents it during the full influence. It will be seen that the heart power indication, was rather stronger during Etherization, than before.

Fig. 5.

Fig. 6.

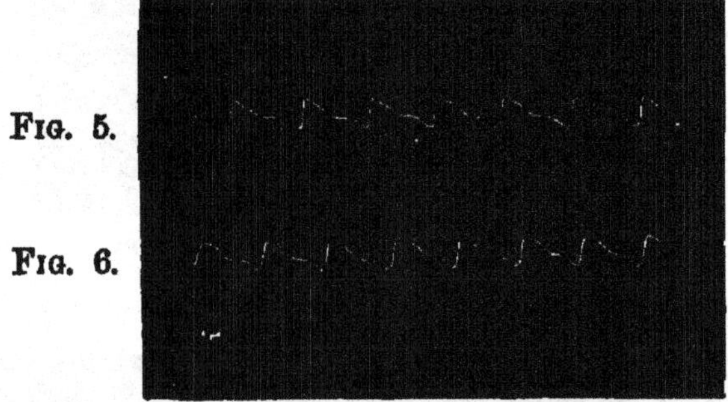

I selected another instance of a female, aged 17, also long confined in bed. The contrast of Fig. No. 7, taken before Etherization, and of Fig. No. 8, during profound Etherization, is notable; the elevation of the pulse line, showing the stimulating property of the Ethereal influence.

Fig. 7.

ig. 8.

Fig. 9. represents the excited pulse writing of a small and nervous female patient, previous to Etherization and operation.

Fig. 9.

Fig. 10. represents the pulse writing of the same patient when steadied by Etherization. The contrast is remarkably favourable.

Fig. 10.

Fig. 11 represents the pulse writing of a healthy young man of 22, previous to operation for artificial pupil—an affection which had not interfered with his general health.

Fig. 11.

Fig. 12. represents the same, when taken under full Etherization and after the completion of the operation. A comparison of this pulse writing with that of Fig. 1. will be ample evidence of the safety of Etherization in its action on the heart.

Fig. 12.

I have taken all but one of these examples as the most unpropitious, occurring in patients of diminished health and vitality, yet it is evident that the most perfect anæsthesia could be invoked under the influence of Ether, with an absolute stimulating effect on the circulation, and that the condition of insensibility could be maintained for a considerable time, yet there was no material alteration of the "pulse writing," and the most perfect sense of security was established.

It is therefore established that—

WHILE CHLOROFORM EXERTS A DEPRESSING INFLUENCE ON THE HEART,

ETHER EXERTS A STIMULATING ONE;

AND THAT CHLOROFORM IS THE MOST DANGEROUS,

WHILE ETHER IS IMMEASUREABLY THE SAFEST OF ALL ANÆSTHETICS.

On the opposite side it has been stated that

The only Argument in favour of the use of Chloroform is that of its being convenient (a).

While the only objections which have been put forward by the Committee as bearing against the use of Ether were the comparatively insignificant ones of "disagreeable odour," that it was "slower," and gave rise "to greater excitement than Chloroform." The odour of Chloroform, it is to be admitted, is sweeter and perhaps the most agreable. Few people, however, dislike the odour of Ether, and whatever objection there may be to the flavour, its exhilarating effects are such that many have found it a seductive substitute for alco-

(a) Erichsen.

holic stimulants, even to the extent of producing intoxication. In Ireland, curiously, its virtues, if they may be so styled in this way, have been already appreciated, and as that province, whose inhabitants are peculiarly accredited with astuteness, has been the most noted for its consumption, we may conclude that it presents, despite its supposed disagreable odour, the recommendation of being "good value" in producing the desired effects; indeed, the intoxicating and stimulating quality of Ether has been known for a considerable time, and a *soupçon* of its use amongst the better classes of society has more or less existed. Mr. Draper (*a*), however, has lately put the question of the "*Use of Ether as an Intoxicant*" in so clear a light that it has attracted considerable attention. He states:—

"The floating idea that there are fair consumers of *Hoffmann's anodyne* and *perles d'ether*, for whom Ether has never been prescribed, quite prepares one for the discovery that there is in the northern part of Ireland a number of people who, forswearing alcohol, supply its place with Ether—a race to whom Ether is what koumiss is to a Kalmuck, ava to a South Sea Islander, absinthe to a certain class of Frenchmen, or gin and whiskey to their more immediate neighbours. That they should take 'nips' of Ether morning, noon, and night, as they would whiskey, and—for anything shown to the contrary—drink good luck or ratify bargains in a glass of Ether, was not a thing to look for, and is, perhaps, without parallel in the history of narcotic stimulants. The facts rest upon the authority of a number of gentlemen, in their respective capacities of physicians, clergymen, ether manufacturers, and druggists."

(*a*) Mr. Draper in the MEDICAL PRESS AND CIRCULAR.

Its Mode of Use.

"The usual quantity of Ether taken at one time is from two to four drachms, and this dose is repeated twice, thrice, or even four and six times daily. It is taken unmixed with water ; indeed, its very slight solubility in that fluid would make this a useless precaution ; but the usual practice is, to take first a mouthful of water, then the dose of Ether, and again a mouthful of water."

Its Effect.

"The intoxication produced by Ether resembles that of alcohol, but is much more rapidly produced, and is more evanescent. The Ether seems to be eliminated entirely by the lungs, and the breath of the ether drinker always affords ample evidence of his addiction to the habit. I am credibly informed that at the fair of Draperstown—which appears to be the paradise of Ether drinkers—the prevalent smell is not, as at country fairs, of pigs, tobacco-smoke, or of unwashed human beings, but of *Ether*."

Its Influence on the Health.

"I have not been able to learn that, apart from the moral ill effects common to all excitants and intoxicants, the habitual use of Ether brings in its train any peculiar evils, and although it would be wrong to draw a conclusion from completely negative evidence, I am disposed to believe that the votaries of ether incur less danger from the habit than ordinary dram-drinkers; and there are two good reasons for this belief. If we assume that there is nothing specifically injurious in the action of Ether, it will readily be admitted that, having a definite chemical composition, and not being very liable to adulteration with other fluids, it must be an improvement upon the sophisticated alcoholic potations, which, with these people, it has replaced. Again, the affinity of ether for water is so slight (*a*) that dehydration of the mucous tissue of the alimentary canal, and that apeptic action which so well mark the difference between the effect of ardent spirits and of alcohol in the form of unbrandied wine, cannot be evils attending its use.

"All the ether consumed in this way is that which is technically termed 'methylated,' that is, prepared from methylated spirit."

The Quantity Consumed.

"Now, if we assume the ordinary quantity taken at one time to average three drachms, and this quantity to be (in stimulant effect the equivalent of half a glass of whiskey, we arrive at the result that three gallons of ether, supply the place of ten gallons of whiskey. It is very difficult to arrive at any accurate idea of the extent to which ether is consumed in the north of Ireland. Omagh is said to take about 400 Winchester quarts (equal to 250 gallons) yearly, and one Dublin manufacturer has sent to Belfast at the rate of 4,000 gallons yearly."

The consumption of Ether in repeated doses appears, therefore, to have had no specially prejudicial effect on the health; while it acts as an intoxicant more rapidly than spirits, it is more evanescent. We may conclude from the experience of the Ether-drinkers of the north

(*a*) 1,000 volumes of ether dissolves but 10 volumes of water.

of Ireland that the vapour may be freely used, and the anæsthetic influence unhesitatingly invoked without having any permanent or deleterious effect, although the system may have been as it were saturated, as it doubtless is by the Ether tippler, who imbibes his two or three teaspoonfuls perhaps six times in one day—an amount more than sufficient to exercise full insensibility by the mere inhalation of its vapour.

It has been stated that Etherization is more tedious than Chloroform in its action. I find this by no means the case. When the time occupied in gradually bringing a patient under the influence of Chloroform, and in proportioning the amount of the Chloroform inhalation to the varying conditions of the pulse and system, are both taken into account, I do not think there will be found much, if any difference in time, when the aggregate of cases is taken; but even if an additional few minutes were consumed (which I do not admit) the *safety* of Etherization will amply counterbalance any inconvenience on that score.

It is to be remembered, that with regard to this question of time, there is a diversity of opinion, and as I have already mentioned, practitioners of eminence and experience (*a*) assert, that, "anæsthesia may be induced by means of Ether as quickly as can safely be done by means of Chloroform." Much evidently would depend on the mode of administration; the aid given by the patient; and the purity of the Ether. I have seen instances where these conditions were attended to, and where Etherization was more rapidly induced, even in *half* the time which had been occupied in the administration of Chloroform on previous occasions, to the same patients.

(*a*) Dr. Lente, Dr. Squibb, Dr. Godon.

The solution of the question of time, appears to be in a great measure dependent on the amount of Ether vapour which is taken by the patient. In the directions given for Etherization it is stated, that some use the sponge or the cone of paper, and it is remarked "that enough air gains admission through the interstices of the (*b*) sponge moistened with Ether held over the mouth and nose." While others arrange the apparatus so as to prevent "the slightest admixture of air" (*a*).

While, therefore, we find it stated that "the admission of air is comparatively of little consequence," that "enough air enters through the interstices of the sponge," and, again, that it is endeavoured "to prevent any, even the slightest admixture of air," evidently there is abundant proof of the *safety* of ether, and of the efficiency of its action. Some of the objections which have been urged against its use, of causing delay, sickness of stomach, headache, or spasm, are dependent on this very diversity of application, as it is found by those surgeons who exclude air that the results are satisfactory in the extreme.

We have here the key of the question. Ether vapour being considerably heavier than air, when applied by the sponge would flow away unseen from the mouth and nose, and much of it thus escape inhalation, while from being concentrated, and more efficiently applied by the other modes last described, it would act more satisfactorily and produce anæsthesia "as quickly as can safely be done by means of Chloroform." (*b*)

The mode chiefly in use for the administration of Ether has been that mentioned in the latest, and in the majority

(*a*) Dr. Lente. (*b*) Asshurst, p. 77.

of the works on Surgery from America (*a*); by using "a thin and hollow sponge, which is large enough to cover the mouth and nose, and which is first wrung out of warm water, and saturated with Ether poured on in quantities of not less than half a fluid ounce; this is laid on, and a cone of pasteboard or light wood superimposed. The first few inhalations should be made when the sponge is a little distance from the face; but as soon as the anæsthetic influence has begun, the sponge may be more closely applied, and need not be removed except when necessary to apply more ether. Of course if, as will sometimes happen, the patient be seized with a fit of coughing, or, from having eaten a meal immediately before the operation, he should begin to reject from the stomach, the sponge must be withdrawn until tranquility is restored. *If the patient breathe freely he cannot be too rapidly Etherized, and there is no danger as in the case of Chloroform from the vapour being too concentrated.* Enough air is drawn through the interstices of the sponge and the perforation of the cone to obviate any risk from this cause, and *rapid* Etherization is much less apt to cause pulmonary congestion than slow inhalation of the vapour, prolonged through considerable time."

Such are the general directions given by a surgeon who avows that he prefers Ether.

I select, in contrast, the directions of a surgeon (Dr. Gross), who prefers Chloroform. He observes as follows:—

Ether.	Chloroform.
During the process of Etherization the patient may sit up with impunity or be recumbent as may suit the	During the process of Chloroformization the patient must lie down, and not only so, but the head and shoulders

(*a*) Ashurst.

convenience of the operator, no injury resulting from even a protracted maintainance of the erect position.

should be depressed, owing to the *greater* difficulty of maintaining the circulation of the brain through the influence of the heart's action.

The admission of air is comparatively of little consequence.

The importance of having an abundance of air during the inhalation of an article so *potent* as Chloroform is self-evident: it is absolutely essential to the safety of the patient.

The inhalation should be commenced with not less than half an ounce, and diligently maintained till full anæsthetic influence is produced, which usually requires a considerably longer period.

The inhalation should be gradually, and not hurriedly, effected, time being allowed to allow the accommodation of the system to its influence, avoiding the shock which might otherwise result to the heart and brain. From six to eight minutes should be spent in producing its full effect.

No special attention need be paid, as the fluid possesses none of the poisonous (!) properties of Chloroform.

The assistant having the charge of the process must give it his earnest and undivided care; and as soon as the inhalation has been fairly entered upon, one of the attendants should sedulously watch the state of the pulse, the respiration, and the countenance.

Effect.

At first a short cough is usually provoked. This soon subsides, and the system gradually lapses into a *calm*,

Effect.

This may be divided into two stages:—1st That of excitement, when the patient struggles and cries. The *quiet* condition, attended with muscular relaxation, closure of the eyelids, and mental unconsciousness followed in many cases by stertorous breathing.

eye has a wild, staring expression, the face is flushed, and pulse preternaturally quick. This varies much in degree and duration. The second stage then ensues, and the individual gradually lapses into unconsciousness. Feeling and intellect are suspended, and if this state be carried further, coma will ensue, and the appearance be apoplectic. As yet all is safe ; but a few more whiffs, and an important link in the chain of life may give way, and the patient be sent into eternity.

The writer lays considerable stress on the importance of using caution, and good Chloroform, and ascribes the *good luck* he has so far had in his practice (though he gives one instance of a narrow escape, where artificial respiration was necessary) to the careful observance of these conditions.

On contrasting the comparative merits of the two anæsthetics as described by him, "*good luck*" is not indeed an exaggerated term when applied to the use of an agent so fraught with danger, and when we find such a suggestive expression used by a writer of eminence, it cannot be questioned that Chloroform, with its signal dangers, has claims far inferior to Ether as a pain-destroyer, and that such a resolution as was adopted by the Massachusetts Hospital—"that the exclusive use of Ether should be an absolute law of the Institution" (*a*)—was most advantageous for the patients.

(*a*) Neligan's "Medecines." By MacNamara.

NOTE.—August 9.—I operated on four patients to-day—one was

MODE OF ADMINISTRATION.

Having referred to the diversity of opinion as to admission and non-admission of air during the process of Etherization, I may state that I adhere to the general correctness of the latter view, and cannot adduce better evidence than the following practical illustration:—

I etherized a medical man, aged about 24, as intelligent and fine a specimen of a vigorous young man in full health as well could be, and who was in agony from toothache. I requested him to notify his sensations as far as possible, and to conduct the administration to himself, as long as he had sense to do so, and to intimate his wants. After the few first inhalations he found it best to desist a little till the throat became somewhat accustomed; he then felt a benumbing soporific influence and called out "more," "more," "delicious," "delightful feel;" he sank into insensibility, the dentist drew the tooth, and he gradually returned to consciousness in a few minutes.

In this muscular young man there was not the slightest spasm, or any unpleasant symptom; there was not the slightest irritability of stomach, and within one hour afterwards he enjoyed a capital dinner. His description from personal observation includes the general rules to be observed—of avoiding irritation at the very commencement, and of then pressing on the influence, to the exclusion of air in a great measure; when this is done there is little apprehension of spasm, or sickness, or of delay.

---

etherized, had two tumours of the leg excised, and was in bed again within ten minutes; another was etherized and had a tumour removed in eight minutes; two others underwent the process in about from six to eight minutes—nothing could possibly have been more satisfactory.

IN CONDUCTING ETHERIZATION THE FOLLOWING POINTS SHOULD BE ATTENDED TO :—

The patient should not have eaten any meal within three to four hours. A glass of wine, or a cup of tea may perhaps be allowed within two hours of the Etherization, unless in cases where stimulants are urgently necessary. If this simple rule be attended to, the instances will be indeed very exceptional, in which sickness of stomach will occur. In eye operations, it is needless to remark, exact precautions should be taken.

The patient must be freed from any tight clothing, and from stays or strings which might in any way impede full respiration. The recumbent position is best suited, with the head fairly raised on a pillow ; lying on the *side* I find better than on the back, but it is a matter of no very great importance ; patients can also be etherized equally well when sitting, but the relaxation of the muscles supporting the head and body leads to inconveniences, and the recumbent position is certainly preferable in all cases.

The inhaler is then charged with from 1½ to 2 ozs. of pure anhydrous sulphuric ether (*a*), which should be poured in slowly. The mouth-piece is then applied gently over the mouth and nose. The patient may hold it and keep it applied for the first few minutes ; this lessens any nervousness about its use, and the mouthpiece can be taken away at pleasure so as to moderate the inhalation and accustom the throat to the vapour. The patient should be directed

(*a*) That prepared from methylated spirit, of ·720 Sp. g., answers well.

to cough or blow out, and as each such action is followed by a full inspiration; such effort aids the breathing in of the vapour very materially, and I am convinced the more freely and fully the Etherization is pressed till insensibility is attained, the better for the patient. After two or three minutes any irritation will be passed, and the breathing will be carried on regularly. The mouthpiece may be then taken charge of by the administrator, and the patient's hands laid down, the breathing will gradually become full, and the stage of insensibility

steadily and equably ensue. The mouthpiece being usually made of elastic tubing, should be pressed firmly on the face, or be slightly moulded to the nose if required; it is well after the few first inhalations, to apply it equably and closely, thus Etherization will be attained more rapidly and satisfactorily. This may be pushed, even till stertorous breathing ensues, which need cause no alarm, but as perfect insensibility is attained without it, it is not necessary further to overwhelm the patient.

The administrator will now suit himself to the circumstances of the case: the patient's condition is altogether in his hands, should there be signs of the ethereal influence passing off, he can pour in a little more, and should the contrary appearances arise, he can, by opening the funnel, allow air to be more or less freely admitted into the inhaler, or he can withdraw the mouthpiece temporarily.

It is best to preserve silence, and not encourage the patient to speak.

If attention be directed to the flexible diaphragm of the inhaler, its motion serves as an index, and an estimate can be always formed as to the condition of the respiration, and how far the patient from timidity or otherwise, is not fully respiring, or the administrator is imperfectly applying the mouthpiece and allowing the escape of the vapour.

Should it so happen that the stomach be sick, and any food have been recently taken, the head should be turned on the side, and the chin slightly depressed, to favour the expulsion of the food.

The ascertained ratio of only one accident been known to occur in 23,204 cases of Ether inhalations, puts the probability of any complication beyond notice.

The operation over, the patient may be allowed to recover gradually, and if the face be sponged with cold water, and the patient soothed when emerging from the influence it will be best.

The time occupied in producing insensibility by the Inhaler varies a little, and some persons seem to resist somewhat more than others. I have seen very many thoroughly insensible in four minutes—others in five; but if eight minutes be taken as an average, it will be found that few cases indeed will exceed it, while the vast majority will fall short of it. *I refer to cases where the Inhaler is used,* as I have comparatively tested the cone and sponge with it, and find that not only is the time much longer, but the effects are far less satisfactory, both as to the temporary and after condition of the patient with the cone and sponge; or, in other words, where a free exposure to the vapour is not effected.

I must here remark that the convulsive stage produced by Chloroform inhalation is not seen where Etherisation is used by the Inhaler, save in *very* rare instances ; nor is sickness of stomach usual, if the simple precaution be taken of not allowing any meal to be given within a few hours of the operation. Indeed, the result of Etherisation cannot be better expressed than by the quotation I have given above from a writer who advocates chloroform :—

"The system gradually lapses into a calm, quiet condition, attended with muscular relaxation, closure of the eyelids, and mental unconsciousness."

When, in addition to these perfect results, it is remembered that it is proved by the hard logic of statistics that *Ether is the safest of all anæsthetics, and eight times more so than Chloroform,* I can hardly conceive that anything further is required to prove its superiority to all other agents.

THE ETHER INHALER

is constructed so as to collect the Ether vapour rapidly, and have it inhaled through the flexible tubing, which, with the mouth-piece, suits any position of the patient.

The respiration is allowed to be carried on freely by means of an india-rubber diaphragm at the top of the instrument, which, by corresponding with each respiration, is self-accommodating. The internal arrangement is such that ample provision is made for the collection of the Ether vapour.

When about being used, pour in *gradually* two fluid ounces of anhydrous sulphuric ether, if for an adult, but proportionably less for a child, and apply the mouth-piece so as to include the mouth and nose. Should the patient not yield in four or five minutes, pour in another two ounces gradually—more will seldom be required, except during some very prolonged operative procedure.

It is desirable to keep the inhaler in the erect position as much as possible.

I am persuaded that any practitioner who employs Ether in the manner I have described will be completely satisfied with the results.

He will also be freed from the incubus of the

DANGERS OF CHLOROFORM.

He can conscientiously advocate with his patient the

employment of an agent which has been proved to be, though hitherto used in an imperfect manner, the

SAFEST OF ALL ANÆSTHETICS.

He will avoid responsibility and the qualms of conscience which, in case of a fatal issue from using the more dangerous remedy, Chloroform, must result to him, indicated in the truthful and touching remark of a practical surgeon when relating the fatal effects and dangers of Chloroform which he himself witnessed ;—

"The use of Chloroform is a serious business, involving as it does the issues of life and death—how serious few can realise, except those who have seen one or more fatal cases ;" and "witness that sad sight when a person lies dead before them, who but a few minutes before was in full possession of life and strength (*a*)."

(*a*) Mr. Greene, *British Medical Journal*, 1872.

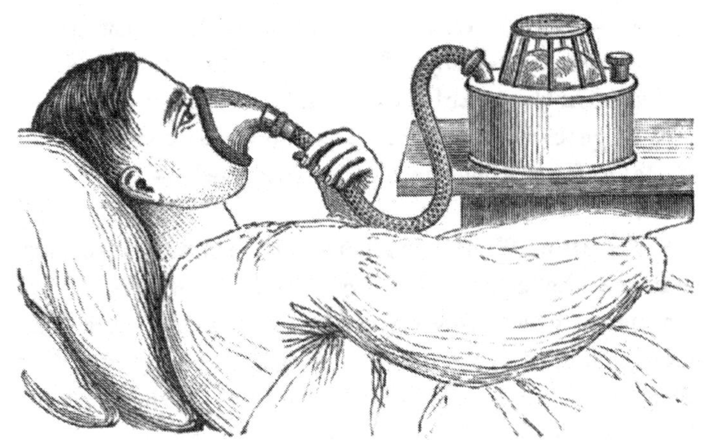

THE SELF-ACCOMMODATING ETHER INHALER.

CPSIA information can be obtained
at www.ICGtesting.com
Printed in the USA
LVOW03s1326150216
475178LV00017B/390/P